DOCTOR WATSON ARCHITECTS

INCOMPLETE WORKS
Volume Four

VICTORIA WATSON

An AIR Grid Publication
Copyright © 2022, Doctor VA Watson

ISBN: 9781838018023

CONTENTS

Introduction, 5
Extract ONE: Plato's Colour Theory; **Leap S01-L01:** Marilyn & Cobra, **6-7**
Extract TWO: Plato on the Real Earth Colours; **Leap S01-L02:** Cobra, **8-9**
Extract THREE: Vitruvius on Colours; **Leap S01-L03:** Vectorah & Cobra, **10-11**
Extract FOUR: Medieval Writers, St Bernard, Hugh of St Victor, Abbot Suger of St Denis, Chrétien de Troyes, St Thomas Aquinas; **Leap S01-L04:** Vectorah-Pink & Vectorah-Green, **12-13**
Extract FIVE: George Ripley, Colour in Alchemy; **Leap S01-L05:** Vectorah, **14-15**
Extract SIX: Alberti on Colour in Painting; **Leap S01-L06:** Vectorah & Chrystophene, **16-17**
Extract SEVEN: Newton's Explanation of Colour; **Leap S01-L07:** Olivia & Chrystophene, **18-19**
Extract EIGHT: Goethe, Colours in the Sky; **Leap S01-L08:** Olivia & Polia, part occlusion, **20-21**
Extract NINE: Goethe, Theory of Colour; **Leap S01-L09:** Olivia & Polia, **22-23**
Extract TEN: Schopenhauer, Colour Theory; **Leap S01-L10:** Polia & Marilyn, **24-25**
Extract ELEVEN: Schopenhauer, Explanation of Colour; **Leap S01-L11:** Polia & Marilyn, part occlusion, **26-27**
Extract TWELVE: Schopenhauer contra Newton; **Leap S01-L12:** Marilyn, side view, **28-29**
Extract THIRTEEN: Chevral on Colour Contrast; **Leap S02-L01:** Chrystophene & Olivia, part occlusion, **30-31**
Extract FOURTEEN: Ruskin on Colour and Composition; **Leap S02-L02:** Chrystophene & Olivia, rising, **32-33**
Extract FIFTEEN: Colour & Expression, Paul Signac, Paul Gaugin, Paul Cezanne, Henry Matisse, Wassiliy Kandinsky; **Leap S02-L03:** Chrystophene 2, **34-35**
Extract SIXTEEN: Colour Contra Space, Henri Bergson, Umberto Boccioni, Wyndham Lewis, Kasimir Malevich; **Leap S02-L04:** Chrystophene & Blue-Chrystophene, setting, **36-37**
Extract SEVENTEEN: Colour and Cosmism, Pavel Florensky, Vasiliy Chekrygin; **Leap S02-L05:** Blue-Chrystophene, **38-39**
Extract EIGHTEEN: Winifred Nicholson, Rainbows and Flowers; **Leap S02-L06:** Green-Vectorah, **40-41**
Extract NINETEEN: C.L. Hardin, Understanding Colours; **Leap S02-L07:** Vectorah, side view, **42-43**
Extract TWENTY: T.H. Goldthwaite, Colour and Evolution; **Leap S02-L08:** Vectorah, rising, **44-45**
Extract TWENTY ONE: Evan Thompson, Colour Hyperspace; **Leap S02-L09:** Vectorah, moving on, **46-47**
Extract TWENTY TWO: Bridget Riley, Colour Events; **Leap S02-L10:** Vectorah & Purple-Vectorah, **48-49**
Extract TWENTY THREE: Stengers & Whitehead, Colour and Eternality; **Leap S02-L11:** Purple-Vectorah, **50-51**
Extract TWENTY FOUR: Paintings by Agnes Martin; **Leap S02-L12:** Purple-Vectorah & Cobra, rising, **52-53**

...What Mies did with colour destroyed 'ideas' and 'influences' with a parodist's precision... Mies's behaviour has the same pattern as humour, considered in context, but it is not funny. What it shares with humour is the element of the unexpected... Kasimir Malevich pointed out that, as things become simpler, emptier, the mind dwells on the little that remains. He wanted to create a 'desert' in which all attention would be focused on this remainder... feeling... The effort to eliminate sensual properties makes one hypersensitive to their presence...

Robin Evans, Mies van der Rohe's Paradoxical Symmetries

Introduction

This volume of Incomplete Works is a compilation of twenty four items, each of which draws together:

1. an extract
2. a Cosmological Leap.

The extracts are reflections on the nature of colour, they are selected from Doctor Watson Architects' library of texts about art, architecture, philosophy and science.

The Cosmological Leaps are reproductions of digital image files, they were produced by Doctor Watson Architects as part of their on-going project that is generically known as Air Grid.

A Cosmological Leap is made inside the computer, to make one relies on the fact, most CAD drawing softwares allow the architect to look at a line as if it were a three-dimensional vector in space. Doctor Watson Architects exploit this facility to build bodies of coloured vectors, drawn together as a lattice structure and looked at on the screen.

Once drawn, a vector body can be posed for a specified point of view and an image can then be captured and exported as a unique file.

It is possible to incrementally move the vector body whilst keeping the point of view static and, by repeating the capture and export process, to compile a sequence of related images.

To make a Cosmological Leap is simply a matter of compiling the sequence of images into a stack, one on top of the other, keeping them aligned in relation to the point of view. At the end of the stacking process a black ground is inserted and the Cosmological Leap appears as the characteristic fluffy colour-form you will encounter as you turn the pages of this book.

(NB another way to create a Cosmological Leap is by treating each image as a movie still and compiling them sequentially to make an animation).

The images shown in this collection were made from a family of six vector bodies, each with its own particular colour spectrum and name. The names of the six are: Marilyn, Polia, Olivia, Chrystophene, Vectorah and Cobra. If you want to know more about them you can look in the publication by Bibliotheque Mclean, whose cover is shown in the illustration below.

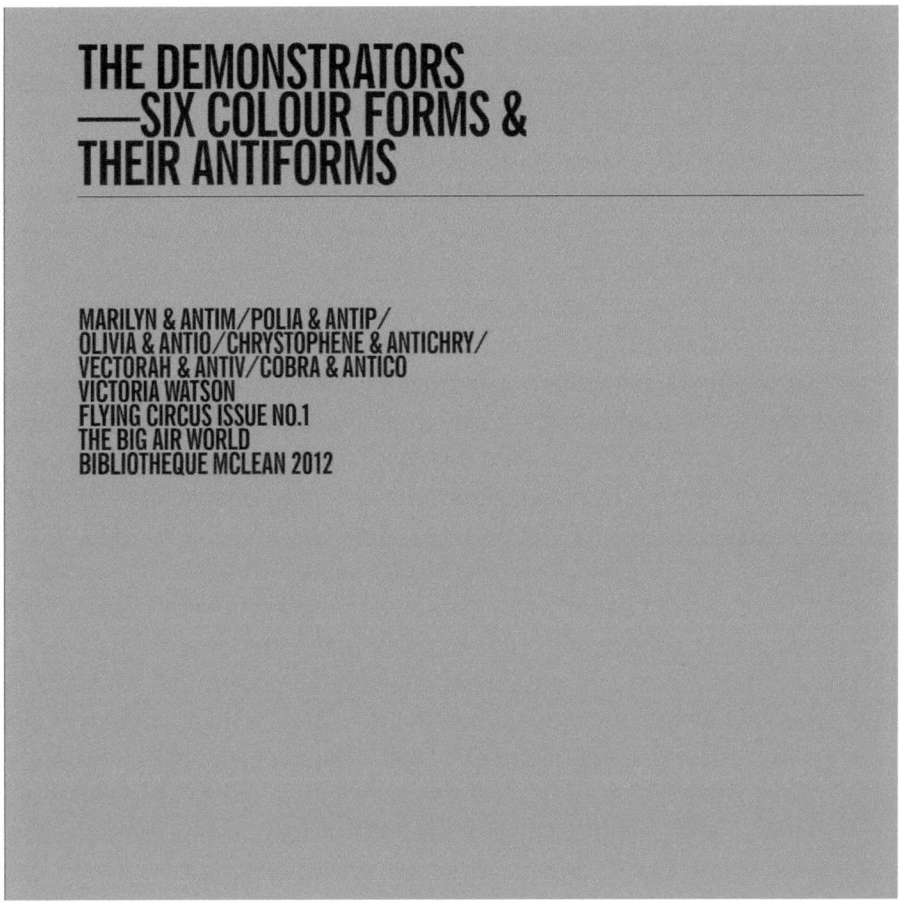

Figure 01
Front cover, The Demonstrators - Six Colour Forms and Their Antiforms, Marilyn & Antim, Polia & Antip, Olivia & Antio, Chrystophene & Antichry, Vectorah & Antiv, Cobra & Antico, Flying Circus Issue No. 1, The Big Air World, Bibliotheque Mclean, 2012

Extract One: Plato's Colour Theory

...There is a fourth class of sensible things, having many intricate varieties, which must now be distinguished. They are called by the general name of colours and are a flame which emanates from every sort of body, and has particles corresponding to the sense of sight. I have spoken already, in what has preceded, of the causes which generate sight, and in this place it will be natural and suitable to give a rational theory of colours... Of the particles coming from other bodies which fall upon the sight, some are smaller and some are larger, and some are equal to the parts of the sight itself. Those which are equal are imperceptible, and we call them transparent. The large produce contraction, the smaller dilation, in the sight, exercising a power akin to that of hot and cold bodies on the flesh, or of astringent bodies on the tongue, or of those heating bodies which we termed pungent. White and black are similar effects of contraction and dilation in another sphere, and for this reason have a different appearance. Wherefore we ought to term white that which dilates the visual ray, and the opposite of this black. There is also a swifter motion of a different sort of fire which strikes and dilates the ray of sight until it reaches the eyes, forcing a way through their passages and melting them, and eliciting from them a union of fire and water which we call tears, being itself an opposite fire which comes to them from an opposite direction - the inner fire flashes forth like lightning, and the outer finds a way in and is extinguished in the moisture, and all sorts of colours are generated by the mixture. This affection is termed dazzling, and the object which produces it is called bright and flashing. There is another sort of fire which is intermediate and which reaches and mingles with the moisture of the eye without flashing and in this the fire, mingling with the ray of moisture, produces a colour like blood, to which we give the name of red. A bright hue mingled with red and white gives the colour called auburn. The law of proportion, however, according to which the several colours are formed, even if a man knew he would be foolish in telling, for he could not give any necessary reason, nor indeed any tolerable or probable explanation of them. Again, red, when mingled with black and white becomes purple, but it becomes umber when the colours are burned as well as mingled and the black is more thoroughly mixed with them. Flame colour is produced by the union of auburn and dun, dun by an admixture of black and white, and pale yellow by an admixture of white and auburn. White and bright meeting, and falling upon a full black, become dark blue, and when dark blue mingles with white, a light blue colour is formed, as flame colour with black makes leek-green. There will be no difficulty in seeing how and by what mixtures the colours derived from these are made according to the rules of probability. He, however, who should ask me to verify all this by experiment would forget the difference of the human and divine nature. For God only has the knowledge and also the power which are able to combine many things into one and again resolve the one into many. But no man either is or ever will be able to accomplish either the one or the other operation...

Plato, Timeaus, 67d - 68d

Leap S01-L01:
Marilyn & Cobra

Quotation Two: Plato on the Real Earth Colours

...For this earth and its stones and all the regions in which we live are marred and corroded, just as in the sea everything is corroded by the brine, and there is no vegetation worth mentioning, and scarcely any degree of perfect formation, but only caverns and sand an measureless mud, and tracts of slime wherever there is earth as well, and nothing is in the least worthy to be judged beautiful by our standards. But the things above excel those of our world to a degree far greater still. If this is the right moment for an imaginative description, Simmias, it will be worth your while to hear what it is really like upon the earth which lies beneath the heavens... Yes, indeed, Socrates, said Simmias, it would be a great pleasure to us, at any rate, to hear this description... Well, my dear boy, said Socrates, the real earth, viewed from above, is supposed to look like one of these balls made of twelve pieces of skin, variegated and marked out in different colours, of which the colours that we know are only limited samples, like the paints which artists use, but there the whole earth is made up of such colours, and others far brighter and purer still. One section is a marvellously beautiful purple, and another is golden. All that is white of it is whiter than chalk or snow, and the rest is similarly made up of the other colours, still more and lovelier than those which we have seen. Even these very hollows in the earth, full of water and air, assume a kind of colour as they gleam amid the different hues around them, so that there appears to be one continuous surface of varied colours. The trees and flowers and fruits which grow upon this earth are proportionately beautiful. The mountains too and the stones have a proportionate smoothness and transparency, and their colours are lovelier. The pebbles which are so highly prized in our world - the jaspers and rubies and emeralds and the rest - are fragments of these stones, but there everything is as beautiful as they are, or better still. This is because the stones there are in their natural state, not damaged by decay and corroded by salt water as ours are by the sediment which has collected here, and which causes disfigurement and disease to stones and earth, and animals and plants as well. The earth itself is adorned not only with all these stones but also with gold and silver and the other metals, for many rich veins of them occur in plain view in all parts of the earth, so that to see them is a sight for the eyes of the blessed...

Plato, Phaedo, 110 - 111

Leap S01-L02:
Cobra

Extract Three: Vitruvius on Colours

...First we will describe the colours which are dug up in their natural state, such as the yellow material which the Greeks called ochre. This is found in many places, also in Italy... Abundant red ochre, also, is extracted in many places, but the best is only found in a few, such as Sinope in Pontus, and in Egypt, in Spain in the Balearic Isles, and also in Lemnos... Paraetonium white has its name from the place where it is mined. In the same way Melian white has its name because a mine is said to occur in Melos, an island of the Cyclades. Green chalk is found in many places, but the best is from Smyrna... Orpiment, which the Greeks call Arsenic is mined in Pontus. Red arsenic also, in many places, but the best is mined in Pontus close to the river Hypanis... I will now go on to describe the treatment of minium or vermilion. It is said to have been discovered in the Cilbian Fields of Ephesus... Malachite is imported from Macedonia; it is mined in places which adjoin the copper mines. Ultramarine (armenium) and indigo (indicum) show by their names the places where they are found.. I will now proceed to those materials which, by special processes, are changed substantially, and acquire the properties of colour. And first I will deal with black... A vaulted apartment is built like a sweating chamber, and is covered carefully with a marble facing and smoothed down. In front of it a small furnace is built with outlets into the chamber, and the mouth of the furnace is carefully enclosed so that the flame does not escape. Resin is placed in the furnace. Now the fiery potency burns it and compels it to emit soot through the outlets into the chamber. The soot clings around the walls and vaulting of the chamber. It is then collected and in part compounded with gum and worked up for the use of writing ink; the rest is mixed with size and used by fresco-painters for colouring walls... The processes for making blue were first discovered at Alexandra; afterwards also Vestorius founded a factory at Puteoli... It belongs to our subject to deal with the production of white lead and verdigris which our people call aeruca. At Rhodes they place a layer of chips in a large vessel, and pouring vinegar over them, they then put lumps of lead on top... When white lead is roasted in a furnace, under the heat of the fire it changes its colour and becomes red lead or sandaraca. This fact was accidentally discovered in a conflagration... We now turn to purple, which of all is most prized and has a most delightful colour excellent above all else... Purple colours are also made by dying chalk with madder and hysginum. Other colours also are obtained from flowers. When the stucco painters wish to imitate Attic ochre, they put dried yellow violets into a vessel with water and boil them... In the same way they prepare whortleberries and mix them with milk, they make a fine purple. Malachite is dear and those who cannot afford it steep blue dye with the herb which is called weld and obtain a brilliant green... Also, because of the scarcity of indigo they make a dye of chalk from Selinus, or from broken beads, along with woad (which the Greeks call Isatis) and obtain a substitute for indigo...

Vitruvius, On Architecture, Book VII, Chapters VII-XIV

Leap S01-L03:
Vectorah & Cobra

Extract Four: Medieval Writers
St Bernard, Hugh of St Victor, Abbot Suger of St Denis, Chrétien de Troyes, St Thomas Aquinas

...We who have turned aside from society, relinquishing for Christ's sake all the precious and beautiful things in the world, its wondrous light and colour, its sweet sounds and odours, the pleasure of taste and touch, for us all bodily delights are nothing but dung... Everything else is covered with gold, gorging the eyes and opening the purse-strings. Some saint or other is depicted as a figure of beauty, as if in the belief the more highly coloured something is, the holier it is...
(St. Bernard)

...Look upon the world and all that is in it: you will find much that is beautiful and desirable... Gold... has its brilliance, the flesh its comeliness, clothes and ornaments their colour...
(Hugh of St. Victor)

...Thus, when - out of my delight in the beauty of the house of God - the loveliness of the many-coloured gems has called me away from external cares, and worthy meditation has induced me to reflect, transferring that which is material to that which is immaterial, on the diversity of the sacred virtues: then it seems to me that I see myself dwelling, as it were, in some strange region of the universe which neither exists entirely in the slime of the earth nor entirely in the purity of Heaven; and that, by the grace of God, I can be transported from this inferior to that higher world in an anagogical manner...
(Abbot Suger of St. Denis)

...The one who went to her behest came bringing to her the mantle and the tunic, which was lined with white ermine even to the sleeves. At the wrists and on the neck-band there was in truth more than half a mark's weight of beaten gold, and everywhere set in the gold there were precious stones of divers colours, indigo, and green, blue and dark brown... The mantle was very rich and fine: laid about the neck were two sable skins, and in the tassels there was more than an ounce of gold; on one a hyacinth, and on the other a ruby flashed more bright than a burning candle. The fur lining was of white ermine; never was finer seen or found. The cloth was skilfully embroidered with little crosses, all different, indigo, vermilion, dark blue, white, green, blue, and yellow...
(Chrétien de Troyes)

...Just as corporeal beauty requires a due proportion of its members and splendid colours... so it is the nature of universal beauty to demand that there be mutual proportions among all things and their elements and principles, and that they should be resplendent with the clarity of form... There are three requirements for beauty. Firstly, integrity or perfection - for if something is impaired it is ugly. Then there is due proportion or consonance. And also clarity: whence things that are brightly coloured are called beautiful...
(St. Thomas Aquinas)

quoted in: Umberto Eco, Art & Beauty in the Middle Ages

Leap S01-L04:
**Vectorah-Pink &
Vectorah-Green**

Extract Five: George Ripley, Colour in Alchemy

...And if you conceive it, both theoretically and practically, By figures and colours, by scripture plain, It wisely conceived, you may not work in vain... Beginning in the first side noted in the West, Where the red man and the white woman be made one, Espoused with the spirit of life to live in rest... Then forth into the North proceed by obscuration, Called the Eclipsing of the red man and his white wife, loosening them and altering them between winter and spring, turning earth into water, dark and nothing clear... From thence by many colours into the East ascend, then shall the Moon be full appearing by day light, then is the purgatory passed, and her course at an end, there is the uprising of the Sun appearing bright, there is Summer after Spring, and day after night: The earth and water which were black be turned to air, and clouds of darkness blown over, and all appears fair... Of how you shall calcine bodies, perfect, dissolve, divide, and putrefy, with perfect knowledge of all the poles which be in our heaven, shining with inexplicable colours, never were a scene more gay... And thus our secret conclusion know without fail, our red man tinges not, nor his wife, until they be tinged, therefore if you will lift yourself by this craft to avail, hide the altitude of bodies, and show out their profundity, destroying the first quality in every one of your materials, and repair anon in them secondary qualities more glorious, and in one glass, and with one rule, turn four natures into one... Pale and black with false citrine, imperfect white and red, the Peacock's feathers in gay colours, the rainbow which shall go over, the spotted panther, the lion green, the Crows bill blue as lead. These shall appear before you perfect white, and many more others. And after the perfect white, grey, false citrine also, And after these, there shall appear the red body invariable, then you have a medicine of the third order of his own kind multipliable... You must divide your white Elixir into two parts, Before you rubify, and into two glasses let these be done, if you will have your Elixir for Sun and Moon do both so, and multiply these soon into Mercury to great quantity, and even if you had not at the beginning enough to fill a spoon, yet may you so multiply both white and red, that if you live a thousand years, they shall stand you in stead...

George Ripley, The Compound of Alchymy, Recapitulation

Leap S01-L05:
Vectorah

Extract Six: Alberti on Colour in Painting

...It remains for us now to speak of the reception of light. In the rudiments we said enough to show what power lights have to modify colours. We explained that, while the genera of colours remain the same, they become lighter or darker according to the incidence of lights and shades; that white and black are the colours with which we express lights and shades in painting; and that all other colours are, as it were, matter to which variations of light and shade can be applied. Therefore, leaving other considerations aside, we must explain how the painter should use white and black... I would like a composition to be well drawn and excellently coloured. Therefore, to avoid condemnation and earn praise, painters should first of all study carefully the lights and shades, and observe that the colour is more pronounced and brilliant on the surface on which the rays of light strike, and that this same colour turns more dim where the force of the light gradually grows less. It should also be observed how shadows always correspond on the side away from the light, so that in no body is a surface illuminated without your finding surfaces on its other side covered in shade. But as regards the representation of light with white and of shadow with black, I advise you to devote particular study to those surfaces that are clothed in light or shade... But we must give some account also of the kinds of colours. So now we shall speak of them, not after the manner of the architect Vitruvius as to where excellent red ochre and the best colours are to be found, but how selected and well compounded colours should be arranged together in painting... I should like, as far as possible, all the genera and species of colour to appear in painting with a certain grace and amenity. Such grace will be present when colours are placed next to others with particular care; for, if you are painting Diana leading her band, it is appropriate for this nymph to be given green clothes, the one next to her white, and the next red, and another yellow, and the rest should be dressed successively in a variety of colours, in such a way that light colours are always next to dark ones of a different genera. This combining of colours will enhance the attractiveness of the painting by its variety, and its beauty by its comparisons... There is a kind of sympathy among colours, whereby their grace and beauty is increased when they are placed side by side. If red stand between blue and green, it somehow enhances their beauty as well as its own. White lends gaiety, not only when placed between grey and yellow, but almost to any colour. But dark colours acquire a certain dignity when between light colours, and similarly light colours may be placed with good effect among dark. So the painter in his 'historia' will arrange this variety of colours I have spoken of...

Leon Battista Alberti, On Painting, Book II

Leap S01-L06:
Vectorah & Chrystophene

Extract Seven: Newton's Explanation of Colours

...I suppose, that as bodyes of various sizes, densities, or tensions, do by percussion or other action excite sounds of various tones and consequently vibrations in the Air of various bignesse so when the rayes of light, by impinging on the stif refracting Superficies excite vibrations in the aether, those rayes, what ever they be, as they happen to differ in magnitude, strength or vigour, excite vibrations of various bignesses; the biggest, strongest or most potent rayes, the largest vibrations and others shorter, according to their bignesse strength or power, And therefore the ends of the Capillamenta of the optique nerve, which pave or face the Retina, being such refracting Superficies, when the rayes impinge upon them, they must there excite these vibrations, which vibrations (like those of a Sound in a trunk or trumpet,) will run along the aqueous pores or Crystalline pith of the Capillamenta through the optic Nerves into the sensorium (which Light itself cannot doe,) and there I suppose, affect the sense with various colours according to their bignesse and mixture; the biggest with the strongest colours, Reds and Yellows; the least with the weakest, blews and violets; the midle with green, and a confusion of all, with white, much after the manner, that in the sense of Hearing Nature makes use of aerial vibrations of severall bignesses to generate Sounds of divers tones, for the Analogy of Nature is to be observed. And further, as the harmony and discords of Sounds proceed from the proportions of the aereall vibrations; so may the harmony of some colours, as of a Golden and blew, and the discord of others, as of red and blew proceed from the proportions of the aethereall. And possibly colour may be distinguisht into its principall Degrees, Red, Orange, Yellow, Green, Blew, Indigo, and deep violett, on the same ground that Sound within an eighth is graduated into tones. For, some years past, the prismatique colours being in a well darkened roome cast perpendicularly upon a paper about two and twenty foot distant from the Prism; I desired a friend to draw with a pencil lines crosse the Image or Pillar of colours where every one of the seven aforenamed colours was most full and brisk, and also where he judged the truest confines of them to be, whilst I held the paper so that the said Image might fall within a certaine compass marked on it. And this I did, partly because my owne eyes are not very criticall in distinguishing colours, partly because another, to whome I had not communicated my thoughts about this matter, could have nothing but his eyes to determine his fancy in makeing those marks. This observation we repeated divers times, both in the same and divers days to see how the marks on severall papers would agree, and comparing the Observations, though the just confines of the colours were hard to be Assigned, because they passe into one another by insensible gradation; yet the *differences* of the Observations were but little, especially towards the red end, and takeing meanes between those differences that were the length of the Image (reckoned not by the distance of the verges of the Semicircular ends but by the distance of the Centers of those Semicircles, or length of the Streight Sides as it ought to be) was divided in about the same proportion that a String is, between the end and the middle, to Sound the tones in an eight...

Newton, Hypothesis of Light

Leap S01-L07:
Olivia & Chrystophene

Extract Eight: Goethe, Colours in the Sky

...These colours correlate closely with meteorological conditions... We must make careful note of the following observation, for it demonstrates the principle underlying every appearance of colour in the atmosphere... A turbid glass held before a dark background and illuminated from the front will appear bluish... The less turbid the glass, the bluer it will look; the least turbid glass will seem violet. Conversely, the same glass held before something bright will look yellow. The denser the glass, the redder it will seem, so that in the end even the sun will appear ruby red... The air, even at its clearest, is a vehicle for moisture and must therefore be considered a turbulent medium. This is why the sky opposite the sun and around it looks blue: the darkness of space creates this effect through the veiling. This is also why mountains in the middle distance seem darker blue than those in the far distance... On the highest mountain peaks the air will seem deep blue because of the purity of the atmosphere there; ultimately it will take on a reddish tinge. In the plains, where the air becomes increasingly dense and filled with turbidity, the blue will grow ever paler, finally vanishing and assuming a completely white appearance. Seen through an atmosphere thick with haze, the sun and the bright area around it will seem to have a yellow-red to red colour... Before sunrise and after sunset, when the sun shines through the thick haze on the horizon, the clouds will be lit with a glow which is yellow or even red... When there is a heavy layer of haze in the upper atmosphere the sun will appear blood red through a very turbid glass...

J.W. von Goethe, Scientific Studies, Chapter VI, Meteorology

Leap S01-L08: **Olivia & Polia, part occlusion**

Extract Nine: Goethe, Theory of Colour

...Let us now proceed by recalling what we stated in the preface. There we considered light as a given. Here we will do the same with the eye. We stated that nature as a whole reveals itself to the sense of sight - the eye - through colour. Though it may sound a bit strange, we will now assert that the eye does not see shape as such, since brightness, darkness, and colour operate together as the sole means for the eye to distinguish among objects or parts of objects. Thus we construct the visible world out of these three elements, and in the process we also make possible the art of painting, an art capable of producing on canvas a visible world far more perfect than the real world... From among the lesser ancillary organs of the animals, light has called forth one organ to become its like, and thus the eye is formed by the light and for the light so that the inner light may emerge to meet the outer light... Here we are reminded of the ancient Ionian school which always placed a strong emphasis on the principle that only things of like nature may recognise one another... None will dispute a direct relationship between light and the eye, but it is more difficult to think of the two as being simultaneously one and the same. We may clarify this by stating that the eye has within it a latent form of light which becomes active at the slightest stimulus from within or without. We can evoke dazzling inner images in the dark through the power of our imagination. In dreaming, we see objects as though in the clear light of day. When awake, we can perceive the slightest impression of light from without, and we even find that when the eye is struck a burst of light and colour is seen... For the eye, colour is an elemental natural phenomenon. Like every other phenomenon it manifests itself in division and opposition, combination and union, intensification and neutralisation, infusion and diffusion, etc., and can best be observed and understood through those general principles of nature... We do not expect everyone to subscribe to this way of thinking about these matters; those who feel at ease with it, as we do, will readily accept it. Nor do we wish to engage later in quarrels and battles to defend it. For the discussion of colour has always brought some considerable risk, a fact that inspired a predecessor to say that waving a red flag before a bull will rouse him to anger, but any mention of colour at all will send the philosopher into a rage...

J.W. von Goethe, Scientific Studies, Chapter VII, Physics

Leap S01-L09:
Olivia & Polia

Extract Ten: Schopenhauer, Colour Theory

...The subject matter of the following essay is a new colour theory, which at the starting point already deviates completely from all previous theories. It is mainly written for those who are intimately familiar with Goethe's theory of colour... Goethe has opened the way for me through a twofold merit. First, inasmuch as he destroyed the delusion of Newton's false doctrine, thereby restoring the freedom of thought about this subject - second - that he delivered in his excellent work in full measure what its title promises: data for a theory of colour. They are important, complete, significant data, rich materials for a future colour theory. He has not, however, undertaken to furnish this theory itself, therefore, as he himself remarks and concedes in the introduction of his Colour Theory, he does not formulate a real explanation of the nature of colour, but actually postulates it as a phenomenon and teaches only how it comes into existence, not what it is... If theory is not universally supported and founded on facts, then it is an empty chimera, and even each single, frayed-but-true experience has much more value. On the other hand, however, all isolated facts from a definite realm of the field of experience, even when they are completely comprised, do not constitute a science until the knowledge of their innermost nature has united them under one common conception, that comprises and contains all that can be found only in those facts to which again other conceptions are subordinated, by means of whose intervention we can arrive at the knowledge and definition of each individual fact at once... Far be it for me to want to pass off Goethe's very well thought out and in every respect throughout meritorious work as a mere aggregate of experiences. On the contrary; it is really a systematic presentation of facts, but it remains thereby... The theory I formulate here will, however, like every true theory, repay the debt of the data to which it owes its origin in that, by trying to explain first of all what colour is according to its essence, all these data now emerge in their proper significance through the context in which they are placed and will be, therefore, again firmly substantiated. Starting from this theory we are even able to judge *a priori* the correctness of Newton's and Goethe's explanations of the physical colours...

Arthur Schopenhauer, On Vision and Colour, Introduction

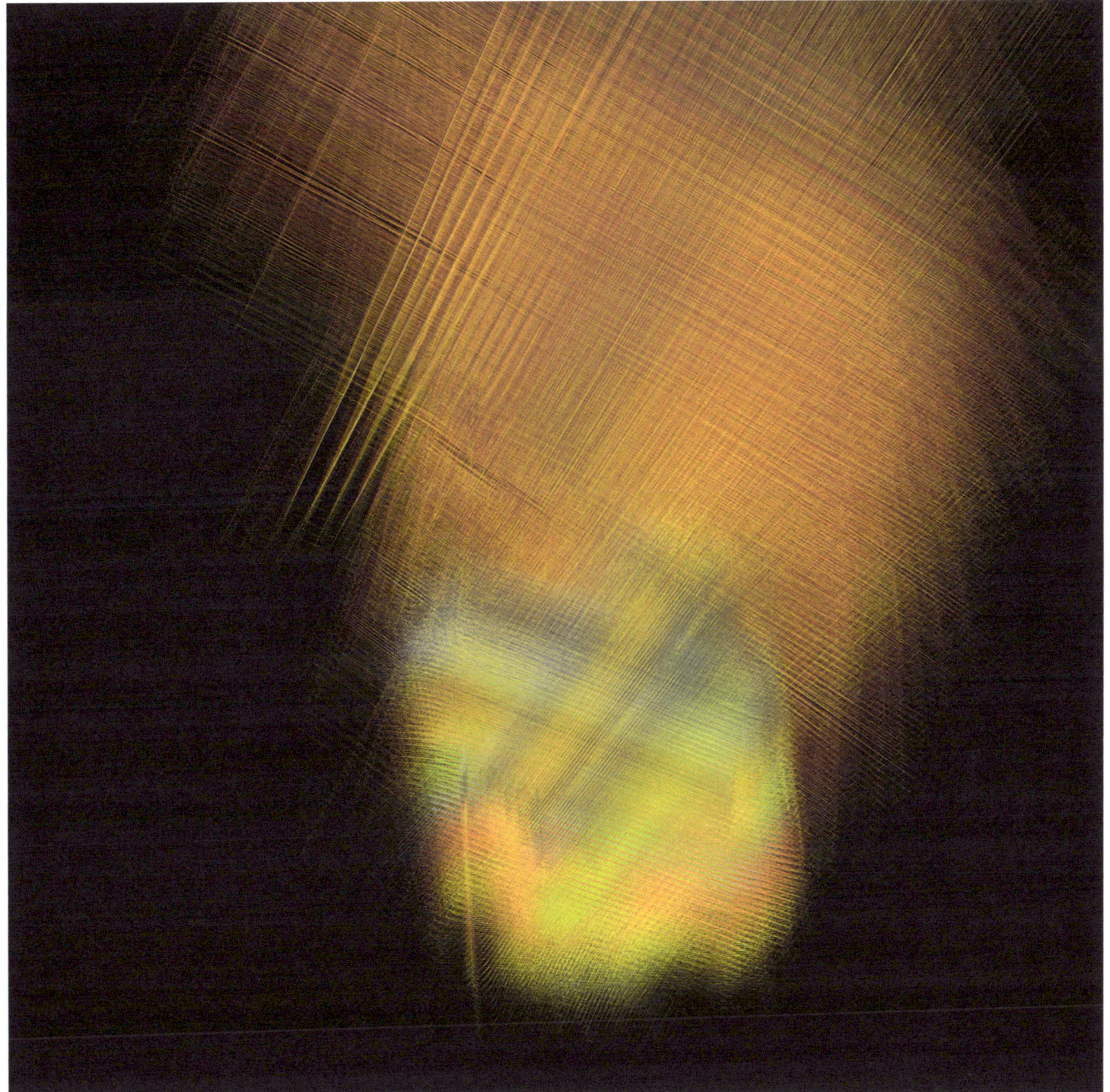

Leap S01-L10:
Polia & Marilyn

Extract Eleven: Schopenhauer, Explanation of Colour

Colour is the qualitatively divided activity of the retina. The difference between colours is the result of the difference between the qualitative halves in which this activity can be divided, and of their ratio to one another. These halves can only be equal once, when they show true red and perfect green. They can be *unequal* in innumerable ratios; therefore the number of possible colours is infinite. Every colour, after its appearance, will be followed by its *complement to the full activity of the retina*, which remained behind in the eye as physiological spectrum. This happens because the nervelike nature of the retina is such that, when the retina has been forced by an external stimulus to divide its activity into two qualitatively different halves, the half that was brought about by the stimulus is automatically followed by the other half after removal of the stimulus. Because the retina has the natural urge to function *to the fullest*, it attempts to restore everything again after it has been torn apart. The greater the part of the retina's full activity a colour is, the smaller the complement of that activity must be. In other words, the closer and essentially - not accidentally - bright colour is to white, the darker or closer to darkness the spectrum that follows will be, and vice versa... The following scheme results from my presentation: Black 0; Violet 1/4; Blue 1/3; Green 1/2; Red 1/2; Orange 2/3; Yellow 3/4; White 1... Black and white are not colours in the true sense, as has always been recognised, because they do not represent fractions, and thus no qualitative division of the retina. They stand here merely as boundary marks to help explain the issue. Accordingly, true colour theory concerns always colour pairs, and the purity of a given colour is based on the accuracy of the fraction that presents itself by that colour. To assume, however, a definite number, for example seven primary colours, existing, realistically, outside of the retina's activity and the ratios of its divisibility, that would constitute together the sum of the colours is absurd. The number of colours is infinite, yet every two opposite colours contain the elements, the full possibility of all the others. This is the reason why, when we start from the three primary chemical colours, red, yellow and blue, each of them has the other two combined as complements. For, colour always appears as duality, because it is the qualitative bipartition of the retina's activity. Therefore, chromatically we may not speak at all of individual colours, but only of colour pairs; each pair represents the totality of the activity of the retina, divided into two halves. The points of division are innumerable, and, as they are determined by external causes, they are in this respect accidental for the eye. As soon as, however, one half is given, the other half follows necessarily as its complement. This can be compared with the fact that in music the keynote is arbitrary, but everything else is defined by it.

Arthur Schopenhauer, On Vision and Colour, Qualitatively Divided Activity of the Retina

Leap S01-L11:
**Polia & Marilyn,
part occlusion**

Extract Twelve: Schopenhauer contra Newton

...He saw that colour is darker than light or white, took for extensive what is intensive, for mechanic what is dynamic, for quantitative what is qualitative, and for subjective what is objective, in that the object of his study was light when it should have been the eye. Accordingly, he proposed that a ray of light is composed of seven coloured rays, in which the colour resides as a *hidden quality* according to laws independent of the eye... That he selected the number seven simply and solely out of affection for the musical scale is beyond any doubt. He needed only open his eyes to see that there are not seven, but only four, colours in the prismatic spectrum, of which the middle two, blue and yellow overlap, and for that reason form green at a greater distance from the prism... That there has been, despite all this, a hunch of truth in the Newtonian error cannot be denied, and follows precisely from the point of view of our observation. We have, according to this point of view, instead of a *divided ray of light*, a *divided activity of the retina*. But, instead of seven parts, we have only two, or then again innumerable, depending on how one looks at it. For the activity of the retina is cut in half with every possible colour, but the points of intersection are, so to speak, innumerable and hence originate the colour nuances which, apart from their pale or dark shades (about which we shall speak shortly) are also innumerable. Accordingly we are being led back from a division of a ray of sunlight to a division of the activity of the retina... An essential difference between my theory and Newton's is also (as already mentioned) that he considers every colour merely as a *'hidden quality,'* one of the seven homogenous lights, he gives it a name and leaves it by that, whereby the specific difference of the colours and the characteristic effect of each one remains entirely unexplained. My theory, on the other hand, informs about these characteristics and makes us understand what the reason for a specific impression and special effect of a single colour is, in that it teaches us to recognise colour as a very definite part of the retina's activity, expressed by a fraction, and further as belonging either to the (+) or the (-) side of the division of that activity...

Arthur Schopenhauer, On Vision and Colour, Relation of the Theory Here Advanced to Newton's Theory

Leap S01-L12:
Marilyn, side view

Extract Thirteen: Chevral on Colour Contrast

...In endeavouring to discover the cause of the complaints made of the quality of certain pigments prepared in the dyeing laboratory of the Gobelins, I soon satisfied myself that if the complaints of the want of permanence in the light blues, violets, greys, and browns, were well-founded, there were others, particularly those of the want of vigour in the blacks employed in making shades of blue and violet draperies, which had no foundation; for after procuring black-dyed wools from the most celebrated French and other workshops - and perceiving that they had no superiority over those dyed at the Gobelins - I saw that the want of vigour complained of in the blacks was owing to the colour next to them, and was due to the phenomena of contrast of colours... I beg the reader never to forget when it is asserted of the phenomena of simultaneous contrast, *that one colour placed beside another receives such a modification from it* that this manner of speaking does not mean that the two colours, or rather the two material objects that present them to us, have a mutual action, either physical or chemical; it is really only applied *to the modification that takes place before us* when we perceive the simultaneous impression of these two colours... *Definition of Simultaneous Contrast...* If we look simultaneously upon two strips of different tones of the same colour, or upon two strips of the same tone of different colours placed side by side, if the strips are not too wide, the eye perceives certain modifications which in the first place influence the intensity of the colour, and in the second, the optical composition of the two juxtaposed colours respectively... Now as these modifications make the strips appear different from what they really are, I give to them the name of *simultaneous contrast of colours*; and I call *contrast of tone* the modification in intensity of colour, and *contrast of colour* that which affects the optical composition of each juxtaposed colour... the modifications of contiguous colours are precisely such as would result from the addition to each of them of the colour which is complementary to its neighbour...

M.E. Chevral, The Principles of Harmony and Contrast of Colours and their Applications to the Arts

Leap S02-L01: **Chrystophene & Olivia, part occlusion**

Extract Fourteen: Ruskin on Colour and Composition

...You ought to love colour, and to think nothing quite beautiful or perfect without it; and if you really do love it, for its own sake, and are not merely desirous to colour because you think painting a finer thing than drawing, there is some chance you may colour well. Nevertheless, you need not hope ever to produce anything more than pleasant helps to memory, or useful and suggestive sketches in colour, unless you mean to be wholly an artist... You may, in the time which other vocations leave at your disposal, produce finished, beautiful, and masterly drawings in light and shade. But to colour well, requires your life. It cannot be done cheaper. The difficulty of doing right is increased - not twofold nor threefold, but a thousandfold, and more - by the addition of colour to your work. For the chances are more than a thousand to one against your being right both in form and colour with a given touch: it is difficult enough to be right in form, if you attend to that only; but when you have to attend, at the same moment, to a much more subtle thing than the form, the difficulty is strangely increased, and multiplied almost to infinity by this great fact, that, while form is absolute, so that you can say at the moment you draw any line that it is either right or wrong, colour is wholly relative... Every hue throughout your work is altered by every touch that you add in other places; so that what was warm a minute ago, becomes cold when you have put a hotter colour in another place, and what was in harmony when you left it, becomes discordant as you set other colours beside it; so that every touch must be laid, not with a view to its effect at the time, but with a view to its effect in futurity, the result upon it of all that is afterwards to be done being previously considered. You may easily understand that, this being so, nothing but the devotion of life, and great genius besides, can make a colourist...

John Ruskin, Three Letters to Beginners, The Elements of Drawing

Leap S02-L02:
Chrystophene & Olivia, rising

Extract Fifteen: Colour & Expression
Paul Signac, Paul Gaugin, Paul Cezanne, Henry Matisse, Wassiliy Kandinsky

...But if this research into the colour and light is not the whole of art, is it not at least one of the most important parts? Is he not an artist who endeavours to create unity in the variety of rhythms of pigments and tones, and who employs his knowledge in the service of his sensations...
(Paul Signac)

...Think also of the musical role colour will henceforth play in modern painting. Colour, which is vibration, just as music is, is able to attain what is most universal yet at the same time most elusive in nature: its inner force...
(Paul Gaugin)

...The man of letters expresses himself in abstractions whereas a painter, by means of drawing and colour, gives concrete form to his sensations and perceptions...
(Paul Cezanne)

...The expressive aspect of colours imposes itself on me in a purely instinctive way. To paint an autumn landscape I will not try to remember what colours suit this season, I will be inspired only by the sensation that the season arouses in me: the icy purity of the sour blue sky will express the season just as well as the nuances of foliage. My sensation itself may vary, the autumn may be soft and warm like a continuation of summer, or quite cool with a cold sky and lemon-yellow trees that give a chilly impression... My choice of colours does not rest on any scientific theory; it is based on observation, on sensitivity, on felt experiences... I simply try to put down colours which render my sensation... In reality I think that the theory of complementary colours is not absolute...
(Henri Matisse)

...Letting ones eyes wander over a palette laid out with colours has two main results: 1. There occurs a purely physical effect, i.e., the eye itself is charmed by the beauty and other qualities of colour... 2... The Psychological power of colour becomes apparent, calling forth a vibration from the soul. Its primary, elementary physical power becomes simply the path by which colour reaches the soul... The love of nature consisted principally of pure joy in and enthusiasm for the element of colour. I was often so strongly possessed by a strongly sounding, perfumed patch of blue in the shadow of a bush that I would paint a whole landscape merely in order to fix this patch... Because I loved colours more than anything else, I thought even then, however confusedly, of colour composition... It soon appeared to me that past ages, having no longer any real existence, could provide me with freer pretexts for that use of colour which I felt within myself... In general, however, I already knew quite definitely at the time that I would conquer absolute painting...
(Wassiliy Kandinsky)

quoted in: Harrison and Wood (eds), Art in Theory, 1900-1990, The Legacy of Symbolism

Leap S02-L03:
Chrystophene

Extract Sixteen: Colour Contra Space
Henri Bergson, Umberto Boccioni, Wyndham Lewis, Kasimir Malevich

...The whole of matter is made to appear to our thought as an immense piece of cloth in which we can cut out what we will and sew it together again as we please. Let us note, in passing, that it is this power that we affirm when we say that there is a *space*, that is to say, a homogenous and empty medium, infinite and infinitely divisible, lending itself indifferently to any mode of decomposition whatsoever. A medium of this kind is never perceived; it is only conceived. What is perceived is extension coloured, resistant, divided according to the lines which mark out the boundaries of real bodies or of their elements...
(Henri Bergson)

...Our growing need of truth is no longer satisfied with Form and Colour as they have been understood hitherto... The gesture which we would reproduce on canvas shall no longer be a fixed moment in universal dynamism. It shall simply be the dynamic sensation itself... Space no longer exists: the street pavement, soaked by rain beneath the glare of electric lamps, becomes immensely deep and gapes to the very centre of the earth. Thousands of miles divide us from the sun; yet the house in front of us fits into the solar disk... The suffering of man is of the same interest to us as the suffering of an electric lamp, which, with spasmodic starts, shrieks out the most heartrending expressions of colour... brown tints have never coursed beneath our skin... yellow shines forth in our flesh... red blazes, and... green, blue and violet dance upon it...
The human face is yellow, red, green, blue, violet...
(Umberto Boccioni)

...We must have the Past and Future, Life simple, that is, to discharge ourselves in, and keep us pure for non-life, that is Art... The Vorticist is at his maximum point of energy when stillest... Our Vortex is white and abstract with its red-hot swiftness...
(Wyndham Lewis)

...Colour and texture in painting are ends in themselves. They are the essence of painting... Futurist paintings and all those of by-gone artists can be reduced from twenty colours to one, and not lose their impression... The subject will always kill colour and we will not notice it... Until now there was realism of objects, but not of painted units of colour, which are constructed so that they depend neither on form, nor on colour, nor on their position relative to each other... I have untied the knots of wisdom and set free the consciousness of colour...
(Kasimir Malevich)

quoted in: Harrison and Wood (eds), Art in Theory, 1900-1990, The Idea of the Modern World

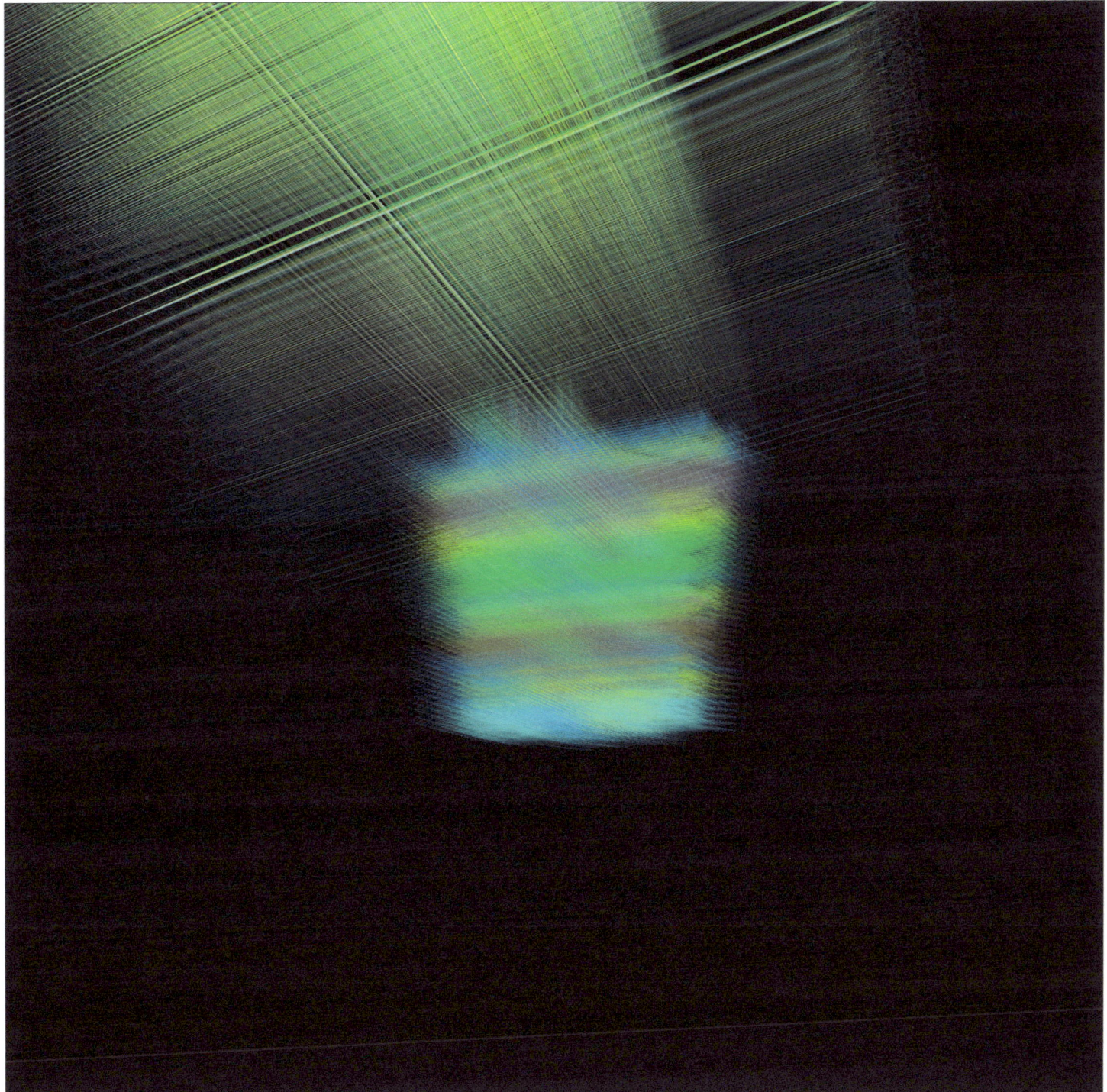

Leap S02-L04:
Chrystophene & Blue-Chrystophene, setting

Extract Seventeen: Colour and Cosmism
Pavel Florensky, Vasiliy Chekrygin

...Calculated to be seen in the play of a flickering flame that moves with every breath of wind, making allowance ahead of time for the effects of coloured reflections from the bundles of light passing through coloured, sometimes faceted glass... Painted under more or less the same conditions, in a half-darkened cell with a narrow window, lit with several kinds of artificial lighting, the icon comes to life only in corresponding conditions... the exaggeration of certain proportions, the accentuation of lines, the profusion of gold and gems the frame and the haloes, the pendants, the brocade and velvet veils sewn with pearls and precious stones... Gold, which by the diffused light of day is barbaric, heavy, and devoid of content, comes to life in the flickering light of the icon lamp or candle, for it sparkles with myriad flashes in every direction, conveying a presentiment of other, unworldly lights, filling a heavenly space...
(Pavel Florensky)

...Great plagues and droughts bring death to many millions of children, men and the elderly, and women, blasting lands rich with colour into deserts... The son of man knows that he is called not to flatten the world's ascent, but to assure that it rise up in unthinkable purity, revealing the colours of the Earth, of all creation, in perfect new freedom and imperishable light... By controlling the course of the Earth, man - pilot of the celestial caravel, celestial warrior of eternal peace, conqueror of the man-beast within himself - becomes a divine artist, readying himself to gather and reunify the living arts - voices, movement, joyous colour - into a single light, a single world, into a life... luminous with colour; his brow, resurrected, comes into focus, and the dead arise, returned to the fullness of life, true beauty, and inexhaustible, immortal force... For the clamour, the oceans' voices, stand before the music of the animated spheres, in which light and sound are one, in which colours are a harmony enlacing and burning with light... Its play is a part of the structure of the Universe; the gathering comet are sealed into force, as are mighty suns, like flashes of brilliant colour woven from logic (higher than flesh) and music... No comfort to him in the plush colours of today - tomorrow is coming on like fate...
(Vasiliy Chekrygin)

quoted in: Arseny Zhilyaev (ed), Avant-Garde Museology, Museum as Common Task

Leap S02-L05:
Blue-Chrystophene

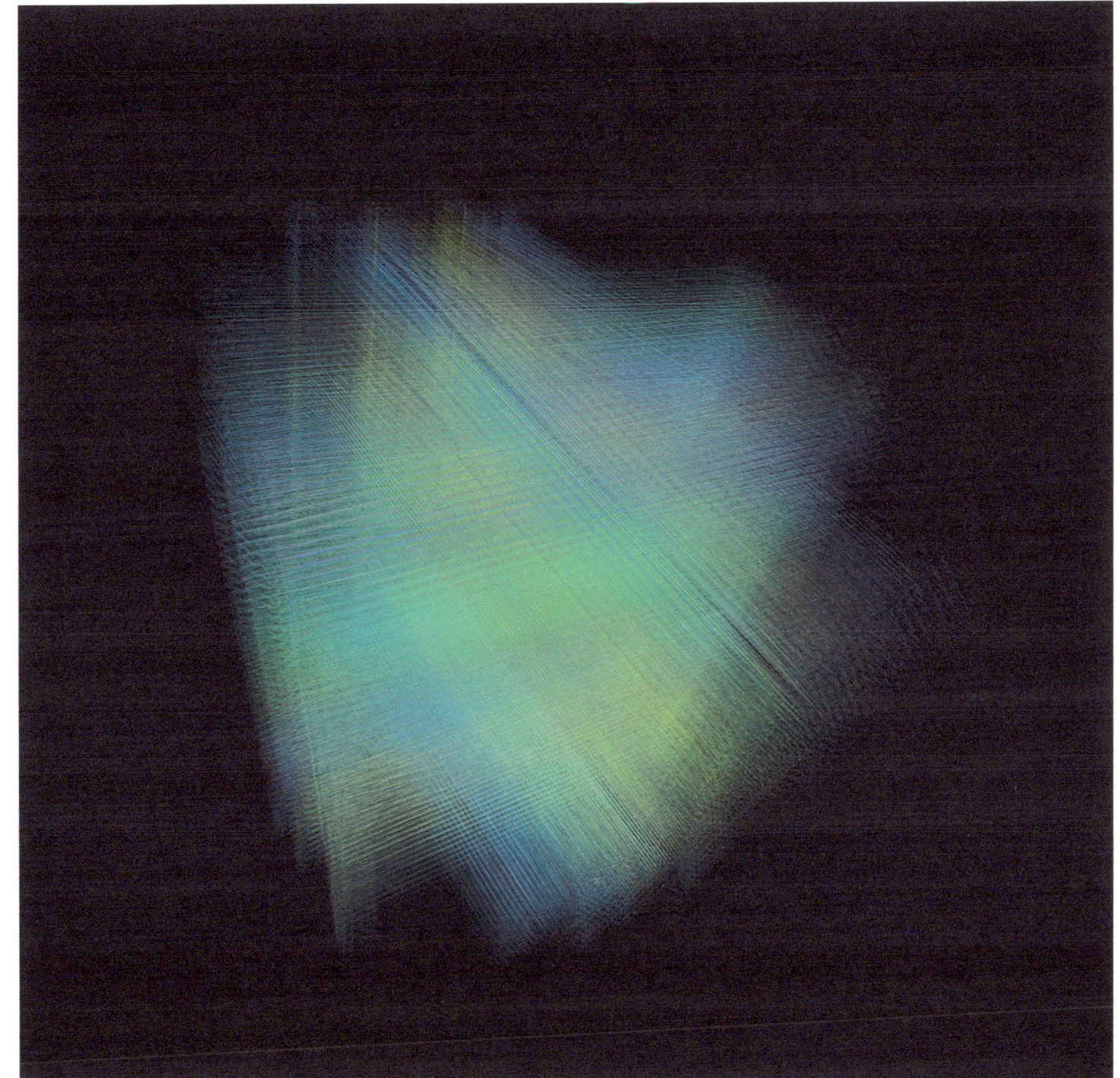

Extract Eighteen: Winifred Nicholson, Rainbows and Flowers

...When I was a Pre-Raphaelite I studied emerald green together with velvet purple... As an Impressionist I studied pink and turquoise in mist and mother of pearl... As an Abstract Constructivist I sought the meaning of yellow against blue - I looked at the hot red of zenith blue in India, I looked at the wine-dark sea in Greece - and then - I tumbled against the pot of gold which is hidden, as we all know, where the rainbow touched the earth - the prism... I found out what flowers know, how to divide the colours as prisms do, into longer and shorter wavelengths, and in so doing giving the luminosity and brilliance of pure colour - in the ordered sequence of the octave of colour... Rose takes all the rays of white light, divides them and keeps them all for herself, except the rose colours, and these she lets us have... How grateful we are to her, and the forget-me-not who sends us back blue, and to violets who let us have violet... My prism is in a black pocket in my purse. I can put my hand into my pocket and pull it out whenever I want to see a rainbow, for the prism shows us rainbows everywhere... How does the prism do that? I do not know. Ask the physicists. They will show you a diagram with long and short wavelengths... Will that help you to paint? Not in the least. For with too many colours, where white touches black and where white hits black you can get into a Delaunay confusion of colours... Then what can you do?.. Select, a Rose and Forget-me-not and Violet select, those wavelengths that you can use, and let the others go... I don't know where the flowers keep their eyes or the prism keeps hers - so that they can divide the colours into the rainbow hues and then let them go and coalesce into the stable colour of an object and surface on to which the colours alight and settle down. But they never belong to the objects or the surfaces - they belong to light: are born of light and die if light dies... But we keep our Eyes in the back of our eyes and can divide and dissect the rainbow so long as we look inward and not only outward...

Unknown Colour, Chapter 4, Unweave a Rainbow

Leap S02-L06:
Green-Vectorah

Extract Nineteen: C.L. Hardin, Understanding Colours

...What is it about colours that seems to obstruct our understanding? They are given to visual experience along with shapes, yet we have no similar difficulties with shapes. A crucial difference seems to be that the essential character of shapes is amenable to mathematical representation, but the essential nature of colours resists it; the one appears quantitative, the other qualitative. Shapes are given to more than one sense, and we are much inclined to suppose that the only sort of characteristics that can be accessible to more than one sensory mode are those which bear structure... But the supposed unanalysability of colours, obvious though it has seemed to many reflective people, does not coexist comfortably with the equally apparent 'internal relatedness' of colours, whereby they exclude - yet intimately involve - each other. There is no variation of magnitude, intensive or extensive, that connects every colour with every other colour. And yet colours are as systematically related to each other as are lengths or degrees of temperature. Red bears on its face no reference to the character of green. Yet red categorically excludes green while at the very same time resembling it in an incommensurably closer fashion than the resemblance of either red or green to any shape or sound... It is the electronic structure of a chunk of matter, particularly the configuration of its atoms' outer electronic shells, which is responsible for its chemical properties. Reflected, refracted, and transmitted sunlight thus carries a great deal of differential information about the chemical condition of material bodies, and it is not surprising that animals should have evolved mechanisms for detecting and exploiting this information. There is nothing in the nature of things which demands that the energy spectrum of the light that reaches the surface of a particular planet from its central star should be tuned to the electronic structure of matter; so colour vision, like complex life itself, depends upon a fortuitous combination of circumstances... The eye has been likened to a camera. This metaphor is apt to deceive, for it represents the eye as a passive conveyer of images to some other more active organ which views them and uses them to glean information about the world... To be sure, the optical system of the eye is camera-like... Unlike a passive camera, the eye begins from the moment its receptors absorb light to transform and reorganise the optical information that comes to it from the world. The retina is in fact, a bit of extruded brain, and by examining those first steps of visual processing which it executes we may hope to gain an inkling of how the brain constructs those chromatic experiences which constitute a portion of its sensory representation of the world...

C.L. Hardin, Colour for Philosophers, Unweaving the Rainbow

Leap S02-L07:
Vectorah, side view

Extract Twenty: T.H. Goldthwaite, Colour and Evolution

...the only information that a photoreceptor cell can report to the central nervous system is that an isomerisation has occurred; information about the wavelength is lost... Wavelength and intensity are therefore confounded. The fact that visual pigments can signal only the rate at which photons are caught is frequently called the principle of univariance... Two conditions must be met for an animal to be specifically sensitive to colour (wavelength). It must possess at least two spectrally different classes of receptor, and it must have the appropriate neural apparatus to compare the outputs of the different types of receptor... The commonest technique in studying sensory capacities of vertebrates is operant conditioning, in which the animal learns to perform a simple task like pushing a bar when it sees the 'correct' stimulus. The successful animal therefore must be able to extract from the stimulus some quality associated with wavelength composition... in principle the animal can be trained to accept light of any spectral composition as being 'correct.' What colours the animal learns will bring it reward are therefore quite arbitrary, implying that its perceptual capacities have at least this degree of flexibility and ability to generalise. In this respect the animal shares a feature of our own visual experience - it sees colours... Colour vision and wavelength-dependent behaviours are distinguished by behavioural tests... To summarize, the behavioural criteria for colour vision imply the presence of processes in which the quality of colour has a perceptual identity. By contrast, the concept of wavelength-dependent behaviour arises from behavioural experiments in which the relation between wavelength and motor response cannot be freely altered by training, implying a neural circuit with substantially less plasticity... the trichromatic colour vision of Old World primates is the most elaborate colour vision system known among mammals... birds and turtles appear to have a rich capacity for colour vision, and in this respect they illustrate what might have been the future of other evolutionary lines. Such was not to be for mammals, for the adoption of nocturnal habits in the premammalian or early mammalian stock probably reduced the number of cone pigments to two, one absorbing in the blue, in the neighbourhood of 430 nm and the second absorbing at longer wavelengths, near 540 to 560 nm... The long and middle wavelength cone pigments of the human retina nevertheless seem to have diverged from each other sometime during the past 65 million years, during the adaptive radiation of mammals... We doubtless do not yet fully understand why this ancestral gene of primates has been such ready grist for the evolutionary mill, but it has enabled these animals to recover a richness of diurnal vision that was largely lost as their ancestors traversed the late Cretaceous...

Timothy H. Goldthwaite, Optimization, Constraint and History in the Evolution of Eyes

Leap S02-L08:
Vectorah, rising

Extract Twenty One: Evan Thompson, Colour Hyperspace

...Human colour vision... is trichromatic. The eye contains three different kinds of cone visual pigments, which are responsible for the fact that three appropriately chosen primary lights are necessary and sufficient to match all the colours that we see throughout the spectrum. Trichromacy is not unique to humans... Many animals are dichromates - squirrels, rabbits, tree shrews, some fishes... others appear to be tetrachromats - goldfish, the Japanese dace, turtles, pigeons... even pentachromats; and it is even possible that some proportion of the female human population is tetrachromatic... Most people when they hear of the evidence for tetrachromatic or pentachromatic colour vision respond by asking what extra colours such vision affords. This question is a fascinating one... it cannot be assumed that tetrachromats and pentachromats would simply see more shades of our colours, that is simply see more particular determinate colours belonging to our colour categories. Although such an ability would certainly be an increase in the sensitivity of colour vision, it is not so clear that it would amount to an increase in the dimensionality of colour vision. Consider that to model the metameric equivalence classes of a tetrachromat requires four degrees of freedom, whereas only three are needed for a tetrachromat. To have four degrees of freedom at one's discriminatory disposal however, is not reducible to being able to discriminate more finely with only three degrees of freedom. To put the point more succinctly and less precisely: seeing in four dimensions is not a better way of seeing in three dimensions; it is simply different. Hence if the issue is what tetrachromacy and pentachromacy imply for understanding colour, then the question to be asked is what the possession of additional degrees of freedom for making chromatic distinctions might mean in perceptual terms... To close the gap between the receptoral level and the perceptual level would require more psychophysical and physiological knowledge of the post receptoral processes involved in tetrachromatic colour vision than is currently available. But by considering in tandem the phenomenal and psychophysical levels of human colour space, and by asking how additional dimensions at these levels would transform the space, we can imagine what a tetrachromatic colour hyperspace might be like perceptually and then take what we imagine as a prediction to be tested experimentally... a tetrachromat's phenomenal colour hyperspace (colour hypersolid) might contain not only colours composed of two novel basic hue components, which would combine to form novel binaries, but also an entirely new kind of hue not found in our phenomenal colour space, namely, ternary hues... These ternary hues would correspond to the additional kind of chromatic distinction available to a tetrachromat, but not to a trichromat...

Evan Thompson, Colour Vision, The Comparative Argument

Leap S02-L09:
Vectorah, moving on

Extract Twenty Two: Bridget Riley, Colour Events

...My paintings are not concerned with the Romantic legacy of expression, nor with fantasies, concepts or symbols... I draw from nature, I work with nature, although in completely new terms. For me nature is not landscape, but the dynamism of visual forces - an event rather than an appearance. These forces can only be tackled by treating colour and form as ultimate identities, freeing them from all descriptive or functional roles... The context of painting provides an arena in which to tap these visual energies - to unlock their true potential and latent characteristics. Once released they have to be organised in new pictorial terms, every bit as much, though quite differently, as when painting nature in landscape or still life... The new motif determines the size, the proportion, even the 'way up' of the painting just as the old natural motif determined these factors before. In working on a painting I choose a small group of colours and juxtapose them in different sequences, to provide various relationships and to precipitate colour reactions. These 'colour events' are delicate and elusive, they have to be organised to make them more *present* - more *there*, more *real*. I take for example three colours, say magenta, ochre and turquoise plus black and white, a situation which then triggers off airy iridescent bursts of colour... I choose a form and a structure in which to repeat these colour clouds, to accumulate them, to mass them until each painted unit is submerged in a visual rhythm which, in turn, collectively generates a shimmering coloured haze. This luminous substance is completely meshed with the actual coloured surface and together they provide the experience of the painting...

Bridget Riley, The Eye's Mind, Working with Nature

Leap S02-L10:
Vectorah & Purple-Vectorah

Extract Twenty Three: Stengers & Whitehead, Colour and Eternality

...When he was finishing writing *Science and the Modern World,* Whitehead conferred a decisive role on 'eternal objects,' a role that would not cease to be redefined in subsequent times... For the moment, the adjective 'eternal' is connected with a contrast. One may baptise what endures with a proper name - each human being, of course, but also a dog, a mouse, or even a mountain... but proper names are not appropriate either for colours or sounds, or for the geometrical objects Whitehead also associates with the mode of experience designated by the adjective 'eternal'... When I say 'it is blue,' but also 'it is a circle,' I am not naming a blue object, or a circular one, but I testify to the ingression into my experience of an 'eternal object'... Whitehead is not mad enough to calmly announce that 'red' as we perceive it existed before the biological invention of the visual organs. This is why he speaks of 'eternality,' a neologism that enables him to avoid 'eternity'... The wonderful world of colours, the mystery of presence, the somber rumination of the mountain testify to the fact that, by the mere fact that it does not share the passage of nature, the object defined in *The Concept of Nature* is no longer adequate for thinking of the order of nature. Colour was a sense-object, and the mountain a perceptual object, taken in a hierarchy that made it explicit that the mountain always has a colour, whereas we can have the experience of a colour independently of what it colours: the famous Cambridge blue. The poets contributed a testimony that raises a very different question, no doubt because their experience is not focused on the urgency of having to decide whether that yellowish shadow is or is not a tiger. And, in so doing, they also forced the experience Whitehead assimilated under the word 'recognition' to diverge: 'it is the same colour' and 'that's my coat' testify to experiences whose difference can no longer be referred to a hierarchy... What is happening... is no longer the event, but what is unification, gathering, in a twofold sense, passive and active. The event not only discloses itself as related to other events: it realizes this relation in and for itself. It happens and passes, of course, but we must first say that... its duration is that of an individualization, of the 'holding together' of the gathering it constitutes. Correlatively, the part is no longer merely included in the whole, and the totality of events 'linked' to a particular event is no longer merely 'signified' by this event. The whole ruminates in every part, and the various parts are henceforth 'presence'... As far as colour is concerned, it is no longer there 'again' but 'once again,' always the same but always new, for it is not worn out, does not live, does not endure. Eternal not because it is always there... but because experience testifies to colour in the sense that it is what it is, without reference to a process within time. Colour is eternal in the precise sense that it requires that endurance and change do not define in an exhaustive way what is required of the order of nature. Red testifies to something that, in nature, does not emerge from this order like all that endures and changes. Red appears 'when it is called,' although the sensation of red requires the endurance proper to the eye and the brain... Red does not emerge from the order to which the eye and the brain testify, but rather the eye and the brain must be understood on the basis of the possibility of the ingression to which the sensation 'red' testifies. The fact of their existence testifies 'for' the eternal object felt as red...

Isabelle Stengers, Thinking with Whitehead, From the Concept of Nature to the Order of Nature

Leap S02-L11:
Purple-Vectorah

Extract Twenty Four: Paintings by Agnes Martin

...'I'm not sure I'm going to keep this one,' she begins. 'I think it may be too worked over.' She turns the painting around and hangs it on the wall. Three vertical stripes, each about 18 inches wide divide the canvas. The two outside stripes are a pale blue and the central stripe a luminous light red. The colour is nuanced, fluid and lyrical, while the white border surrounding the stripes is chalky and opaque. A horizontal central band a quarter of an inch wide divides the canvas, connecting the white borders. It divides the three vertical bands into six rectangles and maintains the visual flatness of the painting. The band prevents reading pictorial space into the subtle brushwork of the colour's application. The paintings that follow are variations in a series of the same colours, many with smaller and more numerous horizontal or vertical units... The paintings are wonders - pale washes of India ink running over a field of white gesso that holds the tracks of horizontal brushstrokes and tiny rivulets of drips running down the surface. The field is traversed by soft graphite pencil lines. The lines are darker than in any previous works but their visual weight is broken by reflected light. The India ink has the metallic quality of liquid graphite and the paintings are lyrical and mysterious... Going through the stack of watercolours, she narrates judiciously. 'This one is flowers - look how delicate that pink is - this blue one is cool - there's very little grey because my last show was grey.' She looks down and points, 'That's a really good line - look at that blue line - there are so many mistakes - that line is too heavy - see that - it ruins the whole thing - I'll have to repaint it.' She continues, 'They are paintings, you know, the same as the big ones - this is one of the few grids,' she says of a pink one. They are pink (really red diluted with water), blue, yellow, orange, grey and the paper's natural colour. Occasionally red and blue lines divide the spaces and sometimes pencil lines do. She says that the subject is joy and happiness...

Arne Glimcher, Agnes Martin, Paintings, Writings, Remembrances

Leap S02-L12:
Purple-Vectorah & Cobra, rising

BIBLIOGRAPHY

Leon Battista Alberti, **On Painting**, Cecil Grayson (trans), Penguin Books, 1972

M.E. Chevreul, **The Principles of Harmony and Contrast of Colours and Their Applications to the Arts**, introduction and commentary by Faber Birren, Schiffer Publishing Ltd, Pennsylvania, 1987

Umberto Eco, **Art and Beauty in the Middle Ages**, Hugh Bredin (trans), Yale Univeristy Press, New Haven and London, 1986

Robin Evans, **Translations from Drawing to Building and Other Essays**, Janet Evans & Architectural Association, 1997, 233-276

Arne Glimcher, **Agnes Martin, Paintings, Writings, Remembrances**, Phaidon Press, 2012

Goethe, **Scientific Studies**, Douglas Miller (ed & trans), Princeton University Press, Princeton New Jersey, 1988

Timothy H. Goldsmith, Optimization, Constraint and History in the Evolution of Eyes, **The Quarterly Review of Biology, Volume 65, No. 3**, September 1990, 281 - 322

C.L. Hardin, **Colour for Philosophers, Unweaving the Rainbow**, Hackett Publishing Company, Indianapolis/Cambridge, 1988

Charles Harrison & Paul Wood (eds), **Art in Theory, 1900-1990: An Anthology of Changing Ideas**, Blackwell, Oxford UK & Cambridge, USA, 1992

Newton, **Texts, Backgrounds, Commentaries**, I.B. Cohen & R.S. Westfall (eds), W.W. Norton & Company, New York, London, 1995

Charles Nicholl, **The Chemical Theatre**, Routledge & Kegan Paul, London, Boston & Henley, 1980

Winifred Nicholson, **Unknown Colour, Paintings, Letters, Writings**, Andrew Nicholson (ed), Faber & Faber, 1987

Plato, **The Collected Dialogues**, Edith Hamilton & Huntington Cairns (eds), Bollingen Series LXXI, Princeton University Press, 1989

Plato's Timaeus, Peter Kalkavage (trans), Focus Classical Library, R. Pullins Company, Newburyport, MA, 2001

Bridget Riley, **The Eye's Mind, Collected Writings 1965-1999**, Robert Kudielkka (ed), Thames & Hudson, 1999

George Ripley, **The Compound of Alchemy**, London 1591

On Vision and Colours by Arthur Schopenhauer and Color Sphere by Philip Otto Runge, Georg Stahl (ed & trans), Princeton Architectural Press, New York, 2010

Isabelle Stengers, **Thinking with Whitehead, A free and wild creation of concepts**, Harvard University Press, Cambridge Massachusetts, and London England, 2011

Evan Thompson, **Colour Vision, A study in cognitive science and the philosophy of perception,** Routledge, 1995

Vitruvius, **On Architecture, Books VI-X**, Frank Granger (ed & trans), Loeb Classical Library, Harvard Univeristy Press, Cambridge Massachusetts, London, England, 1934

Arseny Zhilyaev (ed), **Avant-Garde Museology**, e-flux Classics, 2015

www.ingramcontent.com/pod-product-compliance
Lightning Source LLC
Chambersburg PA
CBHW041820080526

44588CB00004B/66